BOLDLY CANADIAN

THE STORY OF THE RCMP

Written by
Joann Hamilton-Barry

Illustrated by
Frances Clancy

Kids Can Press

Dedicated to the memory of my father — RCMP Inspector Edward F. Hamilton, 1934–93

Acknowledgements

A book like this would not be possible without help from many people, especially my family. My husband, Nick Barry, was encouraging, patient and understanding during the long process. He tirelessly shared his Internet expertise and worked out all of my technological problems. My children, Alex and Hope, were my inspiration. My mother, Norma Hamilton, shared her insight after being married to a Mountie for 34 years. My sister and brother-in-law, Pat Hamilton-Warr and John Warr, read countless pages and helped in so many ways. My brother and sister-in-law, Barry and Jackie Hamilton, offered their support and encouragement at every turn.

Many members of the RCMP took time to answer my questions, and I am grateful to them for their help: A. Commr. Ralph Culligan (Rtd.); Supt. Larry Baker; Supt. Les Chipperfield (Rtd.); S/Sgt. Gary Bishop; S/Sgt. Al Burke; S/Sgt. John MacDonald (Rtd.); Sgt. Brian Culp; Cpl. Don Ash; Cpl. Lee Barnes; Cpl. Fred Fitzpatrick; Cst. Jacques Boucher; Cst. Beth Chipperfield; Cst. Jana Chipperfield; Cst. Richard Hardy; Cst. Nicole Kirker; Cst. Ben McConnell; Force Historian Dr. Bill Beahen; Bob Harris of Justice Institute, Holland College; Rita King; Wendy Kraushaar, RCMP Museum; Bonny Lake; L Division Telecommunications Supervisor Ron Saunders and Staff Historian Glenn Wright. As well, I'd like to thank the staff of the Halifax Forensic Lab and the Charlottetown Detachment for taking the time to give me a tour and for answering my many questions. Dr. Bruce Sealey read part of the manuscript and offered numerous suggestions. D. Commr. William Kelly (Rtd.) responded to my request for information and answered all my questions. Others who proved enormously helpful were Andrew Rodger from the National Archives and Gloria Moor from the *Regina Leader Post*. The staff of Saint John Regional Library helped in more ways than they will ever know. Thank you to everyone mentioned here and to all the members of the RCMP who helped me but wished to remain unnamed. These people assisted me at every step of the way; if there are any mistakes, they are not responsible for them.

Thanks to the staff at Kids Can Press, who cared so much about this project, especially my editor, Liz MacLeod, who made sure I stayed on track and wrote the best book I was able to write.

Kids Can Press acknowledges the financial support of the Ontario Arts Council, the Canada Council for the Arts and the Department of Cultural Heritage.

Edited by Elizabeth MacLeod
Printed and bound in Canada by Kromar Printing

Published in Canada by
Kids Can Press Ltd.
29 Birch Avenue
Toronto, ON M4V 1E2

Published in the U.S. by
Kids Can Press Ltd.
85 River Rock Drive, Suite 202
Buffalo, NY 14207

CM 99   0 9 8 7 6 5 4 3 2 1
PA 99   0 9 8 7 6 5 4 3 2 1

Canadian Cataloguing in Publication Data

Hamilton-Barry, Joann
    Boldly Canadian: the story of the RCMP

Includes index.
ISBN 1-55074-518-2 (bound)   ISBN 1-55074-520-4 (pbk.)

1. Royal Canadian Mounted Police – History – Juvenile literature. I. Clancy, Frances. II. Title.

HV8157.H35 1999   j363.2'0971   C98-932705-1

CONTENTS

CHAPTER ONE

THE RCMP—
Canada's Police

———❈———

"Break and enter reported at a residence at 1 Medley Place," crackled the radio in police car 5B19. Constable Ferguson wheeled his car around and headed through the newly fallen snow to the scene of the crime.

"A sapphire ring, our CD player and about 30 CDs are gone," reported Jack Power, shaking his head. "And we were only out for about 30 minutes."

The thief hadn't made a getaway by car — the new snow showed that the only cars that had been in the driveway were Ferguson's and the Powers'. Then Ferguson looked more closely — there were footprints leading from the house out to the street. They didn't belong to him or to any of the Powers.

On a hunch, Ferguson headed to the town's only bar to see if anyone was trying to sell the stolen items. Several people remembered talking to a man who'd been selling CDs and a ring. They all gave the same description: the man had an odd star-shaped scar above one eye. Cst. Ferguson headed to the bus station to see if the suspect was trying to catch a bus out of town.

On the way, Ferguson radioed his detachment and updated the corporal in charge. A description of the suspect and the stolen items was entered on the Canadian Police Information Centre (CPIC) computer system. Now, any police agency in North America who found the items and made an inquiry on CPIC would learn that they'd been stolen. CPIC also told Ferguson that his suspect's name was Bruce "Starman" Harley. "Starman" had been convicted several times before — for break and enter.

At the bus depot, Ferguson found that a man matching Harley's description had just boarded an eastbound bus. Back at the detachment, Ferguson used CPIC to alert RCMP detachments to the east. Then he arranged with Cst. Baker from the next detachment to meet the bus — and, he hoped, Harley.

Success! Baker apprehended Harley as he got off the bus. Ferguson raced off to meet "Starman" at the neighbouring RCMP detachment. When he confronted Harley with the evidence, "Starman" admitted to the crime. Thanks to the Mounties and CPIC, another criminal was behind bars.

The Queen's Cowboys

The Mounties, the Force, Horsemen, Canada's Finest and the Queen's Cowboys are some of the many names used for the Royal Canadian Mounted Police, Canada's national police force. The red-coated police officer on a black horse is one of the most recognized symbols in the world.

Mounties are everywhere! They work in every province and territory in Canada, as well as around the world. More than 6000 members of the RCMP are involved in routine policing duties such as enforcing the law, protecting life and property, investigating and preventing crime, and maintaining peace and order.

Some of the unusual jobs that Mounties do include canoeing with Prince Andrew, rappelling out of a helicopter onto a moving ship full of smugglers, serving with the United Nations' civilian police forces in Haiti, controlling international crime from the headquarters of Interpol in France, and performing in the Musical Ride.

About a quarter of all police officers in Canada are Mounties. The rest work for municipal police forces such as the Metropolitan Toronto Police, or provincial police forces such as the Sûreté du Quebec.

The RCMP patrols all provinces and territories except for Ontario and Quebec. These provinces had already begun establishing their own police forces before the RCMP came into being. So the main jobs for the Mounties in these two provinces are protecting people such as the prime minister and governor general, working at RCMP Headquarters in Ottawa and enforcing federal laws against organized crime, smuggling and selling drugs.

From the Mounties' beginnings, when fewer than 300 men policed the western half of the country, Canadians have taken great pride in their national police. It has been said that the Royal Canadian Mounted Police is the hardest police force to get into and the easiest to get kicked out of, and that the training to be a Mountie is tougher than for any other police force in the world.

COP CARDS

You may collect hockey or baseball cards, but did you know that some kids collect RCMP cop cards? On the front of each one is a picture of a Mountie. On the back is data such as how long she's been in the RCMP, what her duty is, and any special training she has, such as a pilot's licence.

Police departments use cop cards and cop Pogs to encourage officers to talk to kids. In areas where some children used to be afraid of the police, kids now jump at the chance to talk to a cop and collect a Pog or a card.

HERE'S HOW THE RCMP IS ORGANIZED

Rank	Number at this rank	Rank badge
Commissioner (Commr.) (head of the RCMP)	1	
Deputy Commissioner (D. Commr.)	5	
Assistant Commissioner (A. Commr.)	18	
Chief Superintendent (C/Supt.)	27	
Superintendent (Supt.)	98	
Inspector (Insp.)	255	
Corps Sergeant Major (CSM)	1	
Sergeant Major (SM)	1	
Staff Sergeant (S/Sgt.)	645	
Sergeant (Sgt.)	1585	
Corporal (Cpl.)	2954	
Constable (Cst.)	9517	
TOTAL	15 107	

Where Mounties Work – Detachments and Divisions

About half of all Mounties are based in detachments, where they carry out routine duties. Detachments can have more than 250 staff, such as in Surrey, British Columbia, or only a single Mountie, such as in Sointula on Malcolm Island, British Columbia. There are about 650 RCMP detachments in Canada, as well as smaller satellite and community service offices.

When you walk into an RCMP detachment you'll see a bulletin board with pictures of missing children and Canada's most wanted criminals. Past this area are desks for the constables and clerical staff, and an office for the NCO, or Non-Commissioned Officer, who's in charge of the detachment.

Behind the office area are small rooms the Mounties use for interviewing people, a gun locker where extra weapons and ammunition are safely secured, locker rooms and sometimes an exercise area. Another room is used to test the level of alcohol in the blood of people suspected of driving while drunk. In the next room, fingerprints and "mug shots" are taken.

The lock-up, or jail, is usually at the back of the detachment. Each cell has a bunk, sink and toilet. RCMP jails are used to jail people for only a short time, such as those waiting for a court appearance or "weekenders" serving jail sentences on Saturday and Sunday.

By visiting an RCMP detachment you can gather pamphlets and information about the Force. You may even be able to arrange a tour for your family, class or youth group — call and ask for more details.

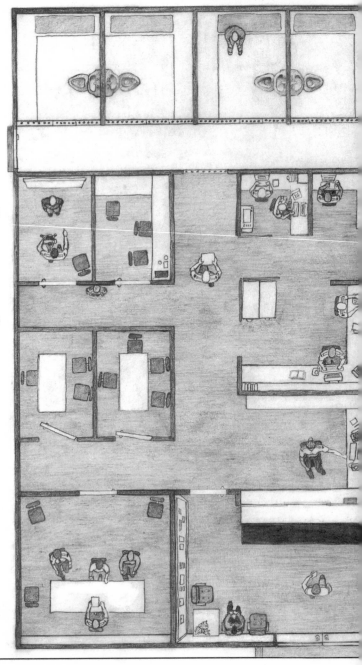

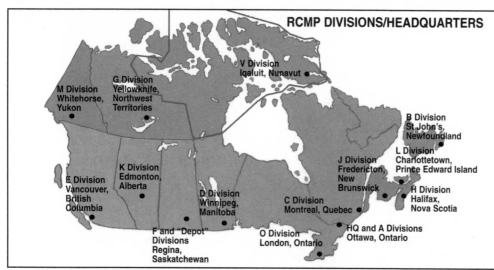

RCMP DIVISIONS/HEADQUARTERS

M Division
Whitehorse,
Yukon

G Division
Yellowknife,
Northwest
Territories

V Division
Iqaluit, Nunavut

E Division
Vancouver,
British
Columbia

K Division
Edmonton,
Alberta

D Division
Winnipeg,
Manitoba

F and "Depot"
Divisions
Regina,
Saskatchewan

C Division
Montreal, Quebec

O Division
London, Ontario

J Division
Fredericton,
New
Brunswick

B Division
St. John's,
Newfoundland

L Division
Charlottetown,
Prince Edward Island

H Division
Halifax,
Nova Scotia

HQ and A Divisions
Ottawa, Ontario

An RCMP detachment is usually located in the centre of the town or community it serves. Each detachment is located within a district. Several districts make up a division and a few divisions form a region. Headquarters for the divisions are usually in provincial capitals. Divisions are identified by letter — check out which division you live in on this map.

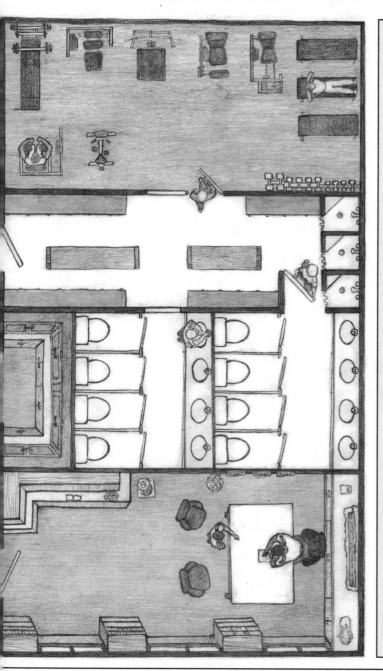

WHAT A MOUNTIE CARRIES ON HIS BELT

You probably know that a Mountie carries a gun on his belt, but did you know that he also carries a mini-flashlight, handcuffs, pepper spray and more? The flashlight helps him see drivers and read ID when stopping cars. The pepper spray can quickly disable a violent criminal. That baton you see expands to three times that size, from 23 to 63 cm (9 to 25 in.).

Mounties used to carry revolvers but now carry semi-automatic pistols. These new guns hold three times more bullets than the old revolvers. They give the Mounties a better chance when facing criminals, who often have more fire power. The ammo pouch holds two 15-shot magazines. With everything on it the belt is heavy, about 9 kg (20 lb.) or about the same weight as a small dog, and can take awhile to get used to wearing.

A Day in the Life of an RCMP Cadet

5:45 A.M.

"Already?! I feel like I just got to bed. It's a good thing I ironed my shirt last night because I barely have time to iron my bed this morning! Can you believe it — we have to iron and put a crease in just about everything, including our sheets and pillowcase. And everybody has to make his bed so that the sheet is folded out over the blanket to exactly the same length. Our instructors say it will help us learn to pay attention to details if we all have to make our bed exactly the same way."

6:30 A.M.

"Time to run down for morning parade, where instructors review the troops. Here, the running is called 'doubling.' And when I say run, I mean run — we aren't allowed to walk or even march yet. Only troops who have learned to march well can actually slow down and march."

6:45 A.M.

"Since there are so many of us, we have to eat breakfast in shifts between 6:30 and 8:00. I just have time to go over some notes before class."

8:00 A.M.

"Police Defensive Tactics is first today. It's a self-defence class, so we learn a combination of judo and karate and how to fight dirty, the way people fight on the street. But we learn more than just fighting. Can we talk our way out of a fight? Or should we use the baton and some muscle? I'm a small guy, so I can move quickly, and I've learned to use this to my advantage when I take on big guys. So many of us get hurt in this class that we call it 'self-destruct class.'"

10:00 A.M.

"For the next few hours I'll be busy learning about Canada's laws, an officer's powers and limitations, and even some RCMP history."

12:30 P.M.

"Lunch! Throwing guys around sure makes me hungry."

1:00 P.M.

"Parade again! The sergeant major looks over the rows of cadets. When he has determined that we are properly dressed and looking like real Mounties, we march or, in our case, run to class."

1:30 P.M.

"My favourite class is driving. Mounties spend more than half of their day in police cars, so we learn defensive driving and specialized skills such as skid training, turning safely and how to stop speeding cars."

4:30 P.M.

"After class I do homework. Tomorrow my friend Malcolm and I have to tell our class how to present evidence in court. That's how we learn here — instructors assign topics and lead discussions, but the cadets teach one another."

5:30 P.M.

"Supper time and I'm starving! We can go back for seconds — and I usually do — but I still miss Mom's cooking."

7:00 P.M.

"Most cadets work on assignments in the evening, or there are always boots to polish. Tonight I'm going to the shooting range but last night Malcolm and I signed out a police car. That was fun — we drove downtown and worked out the fastest routes to the hospitals. We couldn't turn on the siren or stop speeders, but being in a police car made us feel like real Mounties."

10:45 P.M.

"Lights out. Tomorrow's another gruelling day in the training of Canada's Finest."

11

Twenty-Six Weeks at Depot

Depot Division, or the Training Academy, is in Regina, Saskatchewan. This is where cadets train to become members of the RCMP. They are put into groups of 24 people called a troop. Troops used to be all male or all female, but now are all co-ed.

While at Depot, cadets live in one large room or dormitory. Men and women live in different wings of the same building. Two cadets share a small space known as a pit, and the two cadets who share this space are called pit partners. Everything has to be extremely tidy in the dorms. In fact, each pit partner must store everything on her

bookcase so that it's the mirror image of her partner's. Imagine sharing a room with your sister and not only having to keep it incredibly neat, but also having to keep both halves of the room looking exactly the same. If she keeps her pencils in a mug next to her binders, you have to do the same. That's what it's like for cadets.

One of the cadets' most important classes is Applied Police Sciences (APS). Cadets learn how to read people their rights, prepare a search warrant application, make an arrest, perform a search, testify in court and much more. Role-playing and practice situations are used throughout training. At the beginning, the situations are fairly easy. As the training proceeds, however, the cadets face more and more complicated examples.

To give cadets experience at being a Mountie, they must work for at least 2 weeks of their 26 weeks of training at a model village. It's something like a movie set with a house, convenience store, bank, café, travel agency, hotel, RCMP detachment and courtroom. People from Regina volunteer to act in the scenarios that take place in the model village. The instructors brief the volunteers so that they know what

to do to make the job tough for the cadets playing the part of Mounties. Cadets practise being called to the scene of a crime, booking a suspect in a model RCMP detachment, putting the suspect in a jail cell and later taking him to court.

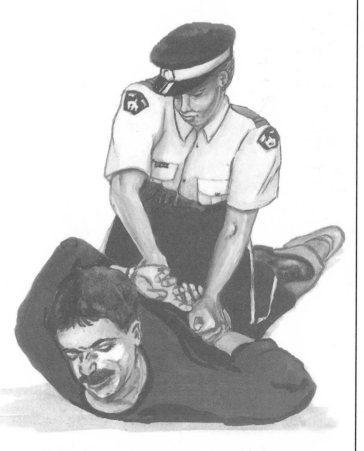

One class that cadets find especially tough is Dismounted Cavalry Drill, also known as Foot Drill or marching. You'd probably find it tough, too — it's difficult to march in exact time with a group of people. Drill instructors haunt the nightmares of most cadets because of their obsession with the smallest detail of a cadet's uniform or the way a cadet walks, runs or tries to march. The instructor tries to develop in each cadet pride in wearing his uniform and being a worthy member of the RCMP.

At the beginning of training the cadets don't dress like real Mounties. They must earn the right to wear the traditional blue pants with the yellow stripe down the outside of each leg — it's known as "getting their marching orders." When they get these pants is determined by the drill instructor.

A threat that the instructor can use after a troop has gotten its marching orders is to take this privilege away. This is known as "pulling their blues" and it happens to almost every troop during training. Fortunately, if the corporal pulls the troop's blues, he usually gives them back in a day or so.

Cadets also learn how to shoot semi-automatic 9-mm pistols, rifles and shotguns at Depot. Once they learn how to shoot accurately, the cadets practise making "shooting decisions" through an interactive computer simulation called Firearms Training Systems (FATS).

The FATS pistols shoot laser beams rather than bullets; cadets see a beam of light that shows how a bullet would travel. By watching the beam, a cadet learns to correct how she is gripping the gun, or if she is flinching when pulling the trigger.

Mounties try to avoid using their guns. Most can go through their entire career without having to fire a shot in the line of duty — but they practise a great deal so that if they have to shoot, they will hit their intended target.

Training is tough. It's unusual for a troop to go 26 weeks at Depot without someone being asked to leave. Cadets who survive their first few months are asked to list the top three locations at which they'd like to start their careers as Mounties. Not everyone gets her first choice, but most cadets are happy with their posting. After all, they will finally be able to put into practice all they have learned in the past half year.

Once at her first detachment, the new Mountie is assigned to a senior Mountie. He will train and help her for a further six months. This last phase of training is called field coaching.

CHAPTER TWO

THE HISTORY OF THE MOUNTIES

Assistant Commissioner James F. Macleod paused on a hill overlooking Fort Whoop-Up. According to all reports it was filled with desperate men who had plenty of guns. They would do anything to defend themselves and their illegal trade of alcohol in this part of the West. These men were here for adventure and money, and they got both by trading doctored whiskey to Aboriginal people. In 1873 the government of Canada decided that these traders had to be stopped. By September 1874, Macleod was on his way to seize Fort Whoop-Up and make the area safe.

Behind Macleod waited nearly 150 men, the first North-West Mounted Police. They were strong and brave but had just been through a gruelling two-month march over nearly impossible territory. If it hadn't been for their guide Jerry Potts, a Métis (half-Aboriginal, half-European) scout with incredible knowledge of the area, they'd never have found Fort Whoop-Up.

Macleod made up his mind — he would not risk his exhausted troops in what could become a bloody massacre. The troops were ready to attack but Macleod decided to give the bandits a chance to give themselves up before his men fired. Not a sound came from the fort. With the brave Potts, Macleod slowly rode towards the fort. Every man held his breath — they could see the two big guns guarding the entrance of the fort and were imagining the hundreds of rifles that were probably aimed at them.

Macleod and Potts made it safely to the fort's front door. When would the fiends start firing, Macleod and Potts must have wondered. Suddenly they heard a sound from inside. The door of the fort slowly opened to reveal — a feeble old man! The bloodthirsty traders had been so scared when they heard that the North-West Mounted Police were headed for the fort that they ran away. The Mounties took the fort without firing a single shot! The tradition of the Mounties always getting their man began with this early success of the men of the North-West Mounted Police.

16

The First Mounties

In 1873 reports began trickling back to Canada's prime minister, Sir John A. Macdonald, that Aboriginal people living in the Northwest Territories (the area occupied today by most of Manitoba, Saskatchewan, Alberta, the Yukon and the Northwest Territories), were being bothered by whiskey traders. So Macdonald created the North-West Mounted Police (NWMP). This group of 300 men would keep the Northwest Territories safe for Aboriginal people and settlers, and make it clear to American settlers that this area was Canada's.

The Commissioner, or commander, of the NWMP, George A. French, gathered the men at Fort Dufferin, near Winnipeg, Manitoba. From there, on July 8, 1874, they headed west. There were no hotels on the route, so they had to take everything they needed to feed themselves and their animals, maintain law and order, and build forts along the way. They marched 435 km (270 mi.) to Roche Percée, near Estevan, Saskatchewan. From there, the weaker men and animals headed 1287 km (800 mi.) north on an easier route to Fort Edmonton.

Three weeks later all the other members of the March West stopped at Cripple Camp, Saskatchewan, where the sick men and horses remained. The rest of the expedition endured extreme hardship. At first the weather was scorching hot, there was little drinking water and the food was terrible. Grasshoppers ate the grass, so the horses and livestock starved. By late summer it was bitterly cold, and the men's uniforms were in tatters.

On September 20 the Mounties were within sight of the Rocky Mountains — they had marched nearly 1370 km (850 mi.).

Then the government in Ottawa ordered the Mounties to establish a headquarters at Fort Livingstone near present-day Dauphin in Manitoba. That meant that some of the men had to turn around and retrace the same punishing route they had just marched.

The rest of the Mounties, under the command of Assistant Commissioner Macleod and guided by Jerry Potts, headed to Fort Whoop-Up, near present-day Lethbridge, Alberta. Mounties soon built Fort Macleod (near Lethbridge), Fort Saskatchewan (near Edmonton), Fort Calgary and Fort Walsh (near Maple Creek, Saskatchewan).

The Mounties rid the area of the whiskey traders and established good relations with the Aboriginal people — all for an average pay of 75 cents a day!

THE FIRST WOMEN IN THE RCMP

Did you know that women have been part of the Mounties for more than 100 years? Back then they guarded female prisoners. Later women worked as technicians or specialists in forensic labs and at headquarters in Ottawa. However, in 1974 women finally joined the RCMP as regular members.

At first, women weren't accepted by all Mounties. Some men felt they'd have to protect their female partners rather than be able to count on them in dangerous situations. But women proved themselves and now work in all areas of the RCMP. Today about 13 per cent of all Mounties are female and the RCMP aims to raise that to 20 per cent.

Mounties Help Settle the West

1882

Canadian Pacific Railroad construction brings more settlers to the Northwest Territories, so the number of Mounties increases from 300 to 500. The Mounties keep law and order; deliver mail; keep records of births, deaths and weather; and even give farming advice. They enforce liquor laws and keep the construction of the railroad on schedule.

1885

FEBRUARY — Métis and Aboriginal people, under their leader Louis Riel, write to the prime minister demanding changes to protect their way of life. It's being threatened by a decrease in the number of buffalo and an increase in the number of settlers. The Aboriginal people on reserves want to be treated better.

The Métis want the government to recognize their ownership of land. Riel prepares his people to rebel because the politicians in Ottawa refuse their demands.

MARCH — Fifty-six NWMP and forty-three settlers are ambushed by Riel's men while marching from Fort Carleton to Duck Lake. Three Mounties and nine volunteers are killed. When this news spreads across the West, other white settlements are attacked. The federal government uses the railroad to rush in troops.

MAY 12 — The Métis surrender at Batoche, near Prince Albert, Saskatchewan.

1890s

Settlers pour into the prairies. The Mounties help the new immigrants adjust to life on the plains.

1896

The Klondike Gold Rush begins in the Yukon. Mounties keep the peace and save many would-be miners from starving or freezing to death by making sure that each gold-seeker has sufficient supplies. Things are very different in neighbouring Alaska, where lawlessness is the rule.

1904

King Edward VII of England honours the North-West Mounted Police by adding Royal to its name, making it the Royal North-West Mounted Police (RNWMP).

THE LOST PATROL

One of the first Mountie tragedies involved the Lost Patrol. Back in 1911, the Force made dogsled patrols between Dawson City and Fort McPherson in the Yukon. The trip was 800 km (500 mi.) long and took about a month.

The 1910–11 patrol wanted to set a speed record, so it took less food to make the sleds light and fast. The patrol was also small, just four men: Inspector Francis Fitzgerald, Csts. Richard Taylor and George Kinney, and former RNWMP Cst. Sam Carter.

The men made good time at first but after 19 days they missed a turn. Days flew by as the patrol searched for the right route. And there were more problems. Despite temperatures of -51°C (-60°F), some of the river ice they crossed had weak spots and the men fell through. Finally they decided to return to Fort McPherson.

Soon the patrol's food was gone. The men began to eat their dogs, although they knew this meant they had to go on more slowly by foot.

Taylor and Kinney became too weak to travel and soon died. Fitzgerald and Carter struggled on for 16 km (10 mi.) before dying. The last members of the Lost Patrol never knew they were only 32 km (20 mi.) from Fort McPherson.

The Force Grows

In 1914 World War I began and Great Britain and her allies, including Canada, went to war against Germany. Many Mounties became soldiers, but those who didn't took on new duties. Canadians had never been involved in such a huge war and were upset and scared. Unfortunately, this made them prejudiced against Germans living in Canada. Many Canadians watched their German neighbours for signs of espionage, even though most were completely innocent.

The Mounties were ordered to arrest anyone of German origin trying to leave Canada — people feared they would join the German army. Mounties also patrolled the U.S.–Canada border to make sure that any Americans supporting Germany didn't enter Canada.

After the war many people were unemployed, while others worked in factories under dangerous conditions. Workers went on strike and Mounties had the tough job of safely breaking up the strikes. The most famous strike took place in Winnipeg in 1919. The RNWMP managed to break it up, but not before one person was killed and many civilians and Mounties were injured.

Winnipeg General Strike

In 1920, the RNWMP began enforcing laws across Canada, so the Force was renamed the Royal Canadian Mounted Police. Its headquarters was moved to Ottawa. In the 1930s the RCMP created a Modus Operandi Section (modus operandi is what MO stands for and it means how a person performs an action), which records how career criminals operate. That makes it easy for police to see patterns and catch criminals more quickly. The Marine Division was created in 1932, the Air Section in 1937.

The Mounties began using cars in 1916, but recruits also rode horses until 1966. In 1972 the RCMP developed the Canadian Police Information Centre (CPIC) computer system. It gives police across the country data about stolen vehicles, missing persons, etc. Women became regular members of the RCMP in 1974. In the 1990s Mounties began international policing in Namibia, Haiti and the former Yugoslavia.

THE MYSTERY OF THE MAD TRAPPER

He killed a Mountie, wounded two others and was one of the most wanted criminals in Canada in the early 1930s. He was the Mad Trapper and most of his life is still a mystery — even his real name isn't known for sure.

The Trapper's story began in the Northwest Territories when a Mountie questioned him about some local crimes. He didn't like the police sniffing around, so he killed the Mountie, and a manhunt was on.

Mounties worked for weeks trying to track down the Mad Trapper; he finally died in a shower of bullets. In his pocket was $2410, about $60 000 in today's money. His pockets also held gold dental work. Since the Trapper's teeth were in good shape, the gold must have come from other people's mouths!

Famous Mounties

There have been many members of the RCMP who have performed above and beyond the call of duty. They have risked their lives, used their amazing detective abilities or performed incredible feats of courage, all to maintain justice in Canada. Here are just a few of the most famous members of this world-famous organization.

Samuel Steele (1849–1919) was one of the first men to join the NWMP. He believed in justice and quickly earned the respect of his men and the people he policed. In 1885 Steele prevented violence during a railway strike in British Columbia. Rising from his sickbed, where the residents thought he was dying, Steele ended a potentially violent confrontation — without firing a shot. Today you can visit Fort Steele, near Cranbrook, British Columbia, and find out more about Sam Steele's career, the NWMP and the people of southeastern B.C.

Jerry Potts (1840–1896) was a Métis who acted as a guide for the NWMP from 1874 to the early 1890s. He spent a lot of time travelling the prairies, developing a keen sense of direction and the ability to observe and recall small details about the land. In his first winter with the Mounties, Potts guided them through blizzards that no other person could have navigated. During one trip, Potts led the Mounties even though he was suffering from snow-blindness.

Major General Sir James Howden MacBrien (1878–1938) was the eighth commissioner of the RCMP. He made many changes to make the Mounties one of the best police forces in the world. He raised the standards for joining the RCMP and also made training tougher by adding courses on criminal law, using science to catch and convict criminals. He even added jujitsu. Thanks to MacBrien, Mounties studied with Scotland Yard's detectives and a Crime Detection Lab was set up in Regina. MacBrien also started the Fingerprint Section, opened a police dog training school and formed the Air Section.

"Doc" McGill (1882–1959) was an honorary RCMP surgeon — and a woman. Frances McGill was a pathologist, which means that she specialized in figuring out how people died. She was so good at solving cases that the RCMP sent her all over Saskatchewan, sometimes on dogsleds and bush planes. McGill was one of the first female pathologists in Canada and one of the first women to teach Mounties. She is the only woman, other than Queen Elizabeth II, to be made an honorary member of the Force.

Constable Alick Pennycuick (1867–1908) was one of the best investigators in the history of the RNWMP. In 1900 this diligent Mountie spent several months painstakingly searching more than 32 km (20 mi.) surrounding a Yukon crime scene. In thick woods he could find bullets, human bone splinters, burnt clothes, keys, a knife, and even a human tooth with lead from a bullet still attached to it. Pennycuick's reconstruction of the crime and his preservation of the evidence resulted in the conviction of a criminal for three murders. Cst. Pennycuick's perseverance and attention to detail set the standard for future Mounties.

CHAPTER THREE

SPECIAL SECTIONS—
In the Field

"That's odd," Constable MacDonald said to herself as she patrolled in her car late one night. "There isn't usually a light on in that shop at this hour."

MacDonald was about to knock on the door when she noticed the lock had been broken off and the door was open. What a mess — the whole shop had been trashed. MacDonald raced to her car to radio the detachment.

Soon, two other Mounties and the shop owner arrived. Carefully they entered the store. The owner reported that he had put his day's earnings in a locked box that was now gone. Who had stolen it? Cst. MacDonald knew she needed special help to solve this case. She knew who to call.

Corporal Mike Dubkowski had just fallen asleep when the call came in. But sleep would have to wait — RCMP dog handlers and their dogs are on call 24 hours a day. Within minutes, Dubkowski and his police service dog, Fury, were on their way to the scene of the crime. While Dubkowski was briefed about the theft, Fury whined with impatience. Soon Dubkowski had him sniffing around the

building, trying to pick up the smell of the thief. Before long, Fury had the scent. Now it was time to start tracking.

Dubkowski had to run to keep up with Fury. First the dog led him through a field, then along a railroad track. There had been rain earlier in the day but the wet grass didn't affect Fury's ability to track.

Suddenly Fury darted off the tracks and stopped. Dubkowski reached down into the long grass — and pulled out what looked like the metal box from the store! The money was gone, but what a clue. Dubkowski gave Fury a pat and then they climbed back to the railway tracks. Fury ran along a little farther, then turned and almost galloped to a nearby house.

A woman answered Dubkowski's knock. As they spoke, he noticed that beside the door were a jacket bearing the name of the local high school and a wet pair of men's boots. Dubkowski asked to speak to the woman's son. When the young man was confronted with the cash box and the fact that Fury had tracked him from the shop, he confessed. Fury had done his job again. Maybe now Dubkowski would get some sleep.

Police Dogs

You may think that dogs have always helped out the RCMP, but dogs didn't become Mounties until 1935. That's when three German shepherds joined the Force. Police service dogs rescue drowning children, find people lost in woods and perform regular police duties, including finding hidden objects, searching for and holding suspects, and defending their handlers.

To become Mounties, dogs attend school in Innisfail, Alberta. Human Mounties go there to be trained, too. To become a dog handler, a Mountie must have been with the RCMP for at least 4 years, then take an 18-week basic dog handler course. Mountie and dog are usually paired up before the start of the course because it's important that they develop a strong bond with each other. Working together, the handler and dog learn about tracking, catching criminals and searching for people, drugs, weapons and explosives. Some dogs are even trained to be lowered from moving helicopters with Emergency Response Team members.

German shepherds and Belgian malinois make the best RCMP dogs because they can work for several hours straight, no matter what the weather's like, they can run up to 50 km/h (30 m.p.h.), and they are strong and

smart. Male dogs seem to work out better than females since the males tend to be more aggressive. Recruit dogs are evaluated to see how quickly they learn, how good their sense of smell is, how they react to strangers, how good they are at retrieving items and how they react to loud noises, such as gunshots. Police dogs usually begin their training when they are 12 to 18 months old. They continue to work for 7 to 9 years.

Like all police work, a Mountie dog's job can be very dangerous. Since 1935, many RCMP service dogs have been killed while on duty, and two Mounties have lost their lives while tracking armed suspects with their dogs.

AIRING AND INDICATING

German shepherds have more than 200 million scent cells in their noses, compared to about 5 million in humans. With their sensitive sniffers, police dogs can detect smells that can help them find lost children or sniff out bombs in airports. If a dog loses the scent, he will lift his nose to try to get a trace of the smell in the breeze. This is known as airing.

When a dog finds something important, he has to find a way to tell his handler. This is called giving an indication and can include a particular bark, a special jump or a different look that the dog gives the handler. The handler must watch her dog closely while tracking so she doesn't miss the dog's indication.

Mounties on Land, on Sea and in the Air

You've probably seen Mounties in their police cars, but did you know that Mounties have a lot of other ways to get around? Not only does the RCMP own 5600 cars, but it also has 2350 trucks, 481 small snowmobiles, 181 all-terrain vehicles, 34 motorcycles, 27 tractors, 4 armoured vehicles, 3 buses and 1 railway car.

Mounties patrol both the east and west coasts in 5 large patrol vessels and are on Canada's rivers and lakes in 377 smaller vessels. The most famous ship in RCMP history is the *St. Roch*. She was the first ship to ever sail across the top of Canada from the Pacific to the Atlantic Ocean.

The *St. Roch's* trip began in Vancouver in 1940 and took 28 months because the ship was frozen in ice for all but several weeks during the brief Arctic summers. When she sailed from Vancouver to Halifax via the Panama Canal in 1954, the *St. Roch* became the first ship to sail around North America. You can now see the *St. Roch* at the Vancouver Maritime Museum.

The RCMP operates 20 airplanes and 9 helicopters, too. Pilots often solve crimes using Forward Looking Infrared (FLIR) equipment, which is mounted on the underside of helicopters. This equipment detects differences in temperatures between a person or object and the surroundings and displays this as a picture. FLIR equipment can find people who are lost in woods, direct police on the ground to crime scenes, detect secret patches of marijuana and track fleeing suspects.

Today the RCMP patrols Canadian waters in search of smugglers who try to bring drugs, liquor, cigarettes and even people into the country. Marine Services members also patrol remote coastal areas, where they are usually the only police presence. As well, Mounties on ships are called on to carry out search and rescue operations.

WHY ARE THEY CALLED MOUNTED POLICE?

Before 1916, the Royal Canadian Mounted Police was exactly what the name says: a police force whose members were mounted on horses. The RCMP purchased its first car in 1916 to drive prisoners from the guardroom at RCMP Headquarters to a jail nearby in Regina.

To patrol the border between Canada and the United States during World War I, the Force purchased many cars and motorcycles. By the 1930s most patrols were carried out by car rather than horse. Even though the Mounties loved their horses, they switched to cars — after all, criminals had cars and were able to get away from the Mounties, who had only horses.

Recruits were taught to ride and care for horses until 1966. Since then, horses have only been used for the Musical Ride, ceremonial events or public relations. Some people think that the Mounties' name should be changed to the Royal Canadian Police or the Royal Canadian Motorized Police. But so far tradition has won out and the name remains.

Protecting Queen and Country

When Queen Elizabeth visits Canada, the RCMP's Protective Operations Directorate makes sure that no harm comes to her. The RCMP also provides security for Canada's prime minister, the governor general and top foreign officials. When Canada's prime minister visits another country, he is always accompanied by Mounties.

The Protective Operations Directorate also develops plans for keeping our leaders safe in the event of a war or other international crisis. As well, the RCMP has plans for protecting buildings and facilities that would be vital in an emergency. For instance, if a major earthquake puts a nuclear power plant in danger, the Mounties are ready to deal with the situation.

Another way Mounties keep Canadians safe is by patrolling many airports across the country. If a passenger boarding an aircraft says anything, even as a joke, about a bomb or a hijacking, or if the airport staff feel a passenger is acting suspiciously, they call the RCMP. A Mountie will be there in less than two minutes to check out the situation. RCMP dogs are also used at many of the larger airports to search for explosives.

The Musical Ride

"Hi! My name's Constable Michelle Gallant and I'm a rider in the Musical Ride. I'm a little nervous today because my horse, Nobel, and I are going to perform the Wagon Wheel — one of the hardest moves in the Ride — for the first time. We've been practising it for months and we know it perfectly, I hope.

"If you've never seen the Musical Ride, let me tell you about it. There are 32 horses and riders making beautiful, intricate patterns that often involve us coming really close to one another without touching — even though sometimes we're galloping at full speed. It's tough and sometimes scary. However, all the horses and riders have learned to work well together. But there's no room for mistakes — you have to be where you're supposed to be when you're supposed to be there or you wreck the move and perhaps hurt somebody.

"Mounties have been performing the Musical Ride for over 100 years. One of the other riders told me that the Ride began in 1890. Back then it only took place in Manitoba and Saskatchewan, but now we travel all over the world. Last year the Ride went to England and next month we head to Japan.

"I waited a long time to get on the Musical Ride. After my first two years as a Mountie I took a short basic course in riding and horsemanship and then a six-month intermediate course. The next part was the worst — waiting for a spot on the Ride to open up. I was lucky; I had to wait for only two years, but some Mounties wait up to five years. New members on the Musical Ride used to be initiated by being dumped into a pile of manure — I'm lucky that's been outlawed.

"Let me introduce you to one of my best friends on the Ride — my horse, Nobel. Like all Musical Ride horses, Nobel is black, weighs between 523 kg (1150 lb.) and 635 kg (1400 lb.), is between 16 and 17 hands high, and began training for the Ride when he was three years old.

"See the decoration on Nobel's saddle blankets? That's the brand that was first used by the North-West Mounted Police on

June 7, 1887. We don't brand horses now. Instead, Nobel has his RCMP regimental number encoded on a microchip embedded in his neck, close to the mane. And all the foals born in the same year are given names that start with the same letter of the alphabet. The only letters that we don't use are Q, U, X, Y and Z.

"Each rider carries a bamboo lance that's 2.75 m (9 ft.) long. Learning to control the lance takes a lot of practice because it's awkward and can be dangerous. See the small red and white flag just below the tip of the lance? It's called a pennon. I read somewhere that when wars were fought on horseback, a piece of white cloth was wrapped around the lance just below the point. When a warrior stuck his lance into an enemy, the cloth kept blood from dripping down the lance and making it slippery to hold.

"At the end of a battle, the winning rider would proudly display the blood-stained cloth. When the blood dried, it made the cloth so stiff that it looked as if it had been purposely folded. So now we put many small folds or crimps in our pennons in memory of the battles in which people lost their lives.

"I love riding Nobel, however the best part about being in the Musical Ride is meeting people in the many places we visit. But my job can be really tiring! From May until November I perform in two shows a day — and no matter how tired I am, I don't get to sleep until I've cared for Nobel.

"As well, sometimes I'm on stable duty all night and I still have to perform the next day. I also take part in parades and displays, and I even escorted the Queen once. Although we don't perform the Musical Ride during the winter, we train hard perfecting new manoeuvres.

"It's almost time for the show. One of the last things I do is put a maple leaf pattern on Nobel's rump. I hold a metal stencil against him and, using a damp brush, brush against the grain of his hair. Nobel doesn't mind it, but I always give him a special pat on the nose when I'm done.

"Gotta run! Next time you see the Musical Ride, come visit us in the stables before the performance. We're always busy with last-minute preparations, but we're pleased to show off our horses and answer your questions."

CHAPTER FOUR

SPECIAL SECTIONS—

In the Office

Martie Pierce saw the light turn red at the intersection just ahead but figured she could still speed through. Suddenly she noticed a pedestrian in the crosswalk — but she was going much too fast to stop. There was a sickening thud and the sound of shattering glass as she plowed into the young man. *Oh no, he's not moving*, Pierce thought. *I've killed him! The cops'll be sure to smell the booze on my breath. I've gotta get out of here!*

When Pierce sobered up the next morning she realized she'd not only killed a man, but also left the scene of an accident. *I don't want to go to jail, she thought. I know! I'll make up a story that'll fool the cops.* So Pierce came up with something that she thought would work and hurried to the police station.

There she reported to Constable Gilles Gaudette that her car had been stolen during the night and returned, but seemed to have been in some sort of accident. The windshield was cracked, the driver's side window was broken and there were dents in the front of the car.

Gaudette thought Pierce's story sounded fishy. Not many car thieves are polite enough to return a car they have stolen after getting in an accident. Gaudette logged on to his computer and read the Watch Notes from the previous night. He discovered there had been a hit and run accident in which a pedestrian had been killed. Putting two and two together, he contacted the Forensic Lab.

Lab tests confirmed that Pierce's car had hit and killed the pedestrian. But who was driving the car? Gaudette wondered if he might find evidence in Pierce's apartment that would link her to the accident. So he and staff from the Forensic Lab went to Pierce's home, where they removed a sheet and pillowcase for testing. They also took the T-shirt and jeans Pierce had been wearing on the night of the accident.

The specialists in the Chemistry Section of the RCMP Forensic Lab found six pieces of glass on Pierce's clothing and bedding — and each piece matched the glass from the car window. When confronted with the evidence, Pierce confessed and pleaded guilty to all charges. Another case successfully solved by the RCMP Forensic Lab.

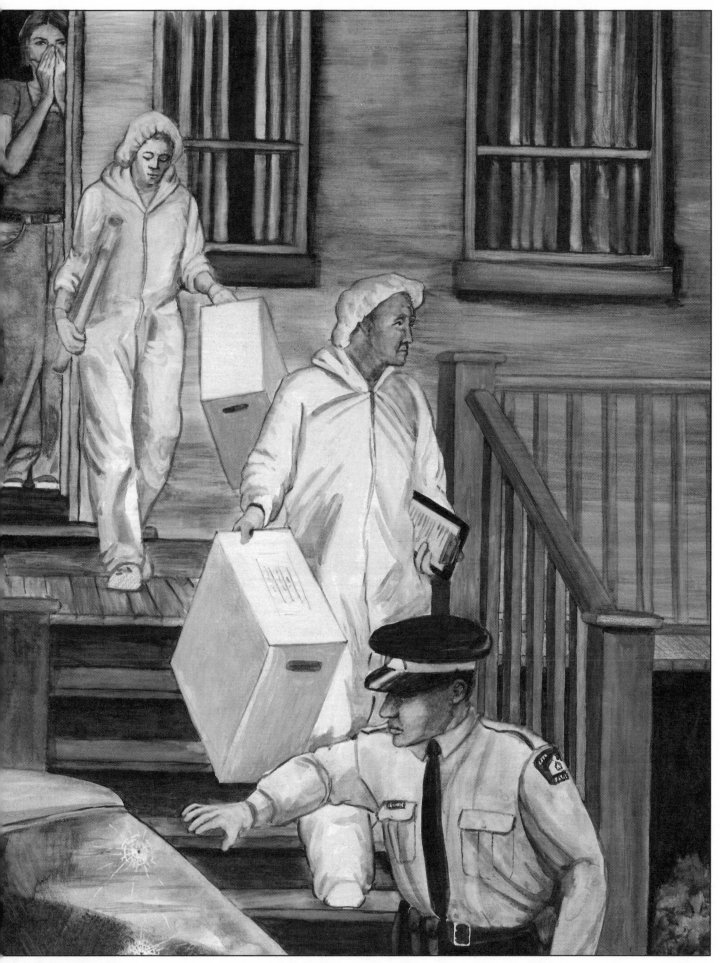

Inside a Police Crime Lab

It's the job of the crime lab to examine evidence found at the scene of a crime to help identify and convict criminals. The evidence can be scraps of fabric, hair, a drop of blood, a fleck of paint, bullets, guns and other weapons, soil or shoes. There are crime labs in Halifax, Ottawa, Winnipeg, Regina, Edmonton and Vancouver. Each one has the first seven sections you see here.

ALCOHOL SECTION

Here, drug and chemical experts examine blood, urine and other body fluids for alcohol or drugs. Mounties come here to learn how to use breath-testing machines that indicate the level of alcohol in a person's body.

BIOLOGY SECTION

This is where samples of hair or body fluid are examined under microscopes or analysed using biochemical methods. DNA typing is also done here. (See page 56 for more information on DNA typing.)

CHEMISTRY SECTION

Staff here spend a lot of time peering through microscopes at glass chips from windows shattered during break and enters, paint flecks from car accidents, remains from a fire, fabric and soil. These experts identify chemicals or other substances found on the samples.

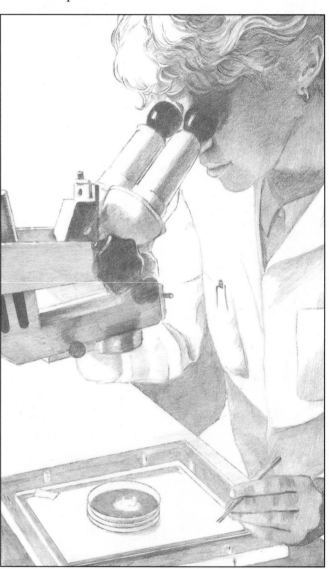

DOCUMENTS SECTION

Was the document produced by a laser printer, typewriter, printing press or photocopier? Were the forged cheques all written by the same person? The staff here can tell you and even say what brand and model of machine created a document.

FIREARMS SECTION

Bullets left at the scene of a crime are tested here to see what type of gun they came from and if they match a suspect's weapon.

TOXICOLOGY SECTION

Staff in this area are poison experts. They test body fluids and tissues for drugs or poisons and figure out the drug's effect.

PHOTOGRAPHY SECTION

When staff from any section in the crime lab need photographs taken, they phone here. Photos of the scene of the crime that are used in court are taken by these experts.

CENTRAL BUREAU FOR COUNTERFEITS

Passports, money, credit cards — they can all be forged, but experts in this section, located only in the Ottawa lab, can almost always tell the difference between a forgery and the real thing.

A LIBRARY FULL OF GUNS

Hung on the wall and in cabinets in the Firearms Section you'll find hundreds of guns ranging from cheap .22-calibre guns known as "Saturday night specials" to machine guns used during World War II.

There are knife blades that look like part of a belt buckle, blades concealed in walking sticks, and martial arts weapons such as throwing stars and nunchaku sticks.

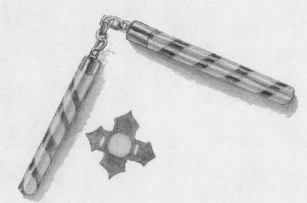

These illegal weapons were all seized by Mounties at the scenes of various crimes. These weapons help specialists here identify and classify other weapons as well as educate Mounties about weapons used on the street.

Lasers, Krazy Glue and the Ident Specialist

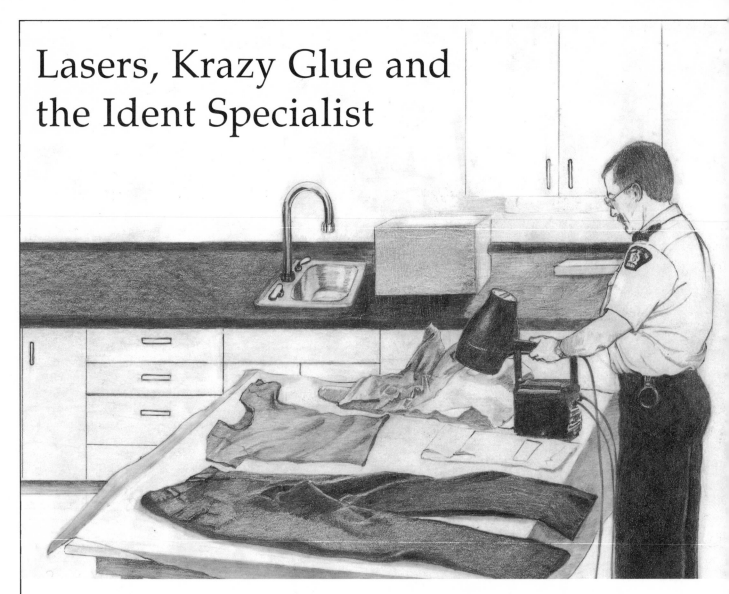

RCMP Identification Specialists are the first officers to examine most crime scenes. Carrying tweezers and wearing white disposable overalls (called bunnysuits) and surgical gloves, they crawl along the floor or ground looking for anything unusual. Evidence is bagged, labelled and taken back to the lab for examination. No one is allowed near the site until the Ident Specialists have collected all their evidence and photographed the scene.

Back in the lab, the Ident Specialists often grab a tube of Krazy Glue. Why? The fumes from heated Krazy Glue can make invisible fingerprints appear under an ultraviolet or laser light known as a Luma-Lite. Finding and identifying fingerprints can confirm the identity of the victim of a crime or prove the guilt of a suspect.

"If a suspect's fingerprints are found on the murder weapon, all over the room and on the victim, chances are he's guilty," says Cst. Philip Leung, an Ident Specialist. "It's amazing what we can see using our Luma-Lite at a crime scene. The tiniest fibre will show up under the laser, and one good fingerprint is enough to get a conviction."

The laser can also be used to detect bloodstains that perpetrators have tried to hide. Blood can be washed away and walls can be repainted, but under the laser the blood traces will show up. "We even have experts in the RCMP who can look at bloodstains and tell from the size, shape,

location, distribution and pattern of the drops of blood exactly what happened," explains Leung. "Others are trained to excavate crime scenes using special archaeological techniques."

The Fingerprint Branch and the Criminal History Branch (CHB) are also part of Identification Services. The Fingerprint Branch collects fingerprints taken by all police across Canada and the CHB keeps files on people with criminal records. For instance, when a Mountie stops a car, he asks the driver for her driver's licence and registration. Back in his police car, the Mountie uses the Canadian Police Information Centre (CPIC) computer system to check the driver's criminal record and make sure that the car hasn't been stolen.

The RCMP has data on more than 2.7 million people, and 12 000 sets of fingerprints are added each month.

MOUNTIES CATCH MARTIN LUTHER KING'S KILLER

It's April 4, 1968, and the United States is in mourning. Martin Luther King, the American civil rights leader, has been assassinated, and the FBI suspects James Earl Ray of the crime. Working on a hunch that Ray is in Canada and may try to use a falsely obtained Canadian passport, five Mounties begin examining the photos on recent passport applications.

Success! After working for a month and looking at 250 000 applications, one of the team notices a picture that looks like Ray. The Mounties quickly discover that he is using an alias and has booked a flight to Europe. Thanks to the RCMP, the FBI eventually arrests and convicts Ray.

Bombs and the Mounties

Dismantling bombs can be deadly, and nobody knows that better than the RCMP's Explosive Technicians. They work behind protective shields, wear armoured bomb suits and operate robot-like devices to dismantle bombs from a safe distance. Sometimes Explosive Disposal and Response Units (EDU) detonate a bomb on purpose — but they do it by remote control using a laser, under safe conditions.

About 75 Mounties are trained to dismantle bombs and are known as Police Explosive Technicians. All regular members of the RCMP are given some training in explosives at Depot in Regina. But Police Explosive Technicians receive at least nine weeks of intensive training and additional training to keep them up to date. They respond to more than 400 calls each year.

The RCMP also runs the Canadian Bomb Data Centre. All police officers in Canada, no matter what police force they work for, report any illegal use of explosives here. The Centre gives police details about bombings that have taken place. It also keeps police up to date on new devices used in dismantling bombs.

An EDU robot safely removes a suitcase that contains a bomb.

Computer Crime

Some people commit crimes without leaving their homes by using computers and modems. Hackers break into bank computers and put money in their accounts or erase credit card debts. Some change the marks on their school's computer or steal assignments from classmates' computers. A special type of hacker, called a "phone phreak," makes free long-distance calls.

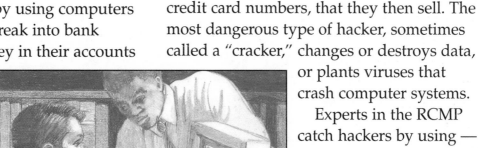

Some hackers steal files and data, such as credit card numbers, that they then sell. The most dangerous type of hacker, sometimes called a "cracker," changes or destroys data, or plants viruses that crash computer systems.

Experts in the RCMP catch hackers by using — what else? — computers. They analyse the use of the telephone lines as well as information provided by the victims to track down the criminals.

FUNNY MONEY

Can you spot fake money? Find one of the tiny green dots on any bill and carefully try to scratch it off. If you've got funny money, you'll rip the paper. As well, some of the print on real money has raised lettering, while on fake money it doesn't.

The RCMP operates the Central Bureau for Counterfeits to track down counterfeit materials. The officers there identify counterfeit money and documents, such as passports, airline tickets and credit cards. They also tell other Canadian police about counterfeit scams, collect data on counterfeit money and the equipment used to make it, and work with Interpol and the U.S. Secret Service. As well, these Mounties educate other Canadian police forces about counterfeit money and train people in banks and businesses.

You probably won't ever get to see counterfeit bills because they usually are discovered quickly. The police catch a lot of funny money before it gets into circulation. How much is a lot? In 1989, more than $2.5 million was seized in a single case.

CHAPTER FIVE

UNUSUAL JOBS

"What?!" exclaimed Constable Patricia Saunders as she read the messages off her computer. "The FBI is looking for somebody who sounds just like our local doctor."

Saunders continued reading the message from Interpol that had been sent out on the Canadian Police Information Centre (CPIC) computer system. The name of the criminal was different from the doctor's but the physical description and other details matched exactly.

Dr. Roberts and his family kept pretty much to themselves, but they had been in town for two years now and were well liked. However, Cst. Saunders knew her duty. With a copy of the message in her hand, she went to speak with her corporal.

A few hours later, Cst. Saunders and another Mountie visited Dr. Roberts at his home and confronted him with the facts they had uncovered. He had attended the same medical school and had worked in the same places as

the doctor wanted by the FBI. The doctors' descriptions matched and so did their birth dates.

Dr. Roberts knew he had been found out and confessed all to the Mounties. He explained that he had tried to pay off his medical school bills by gambling. Big losses led to fraud and cheating on his income tax. Dr. Roberts had been caught, but while waiting to be sentenced for his crime, he and his family left the U.S. and headed for a small town in Canada.

Douglas Robert Stewart, the doctor's real identity, was escorted to RCMP Headquarters for further questioning. He was held there until two FBI agents arrived to escort him back to the United States to serve his prison time. Shortly afterwards, the Roberts family left town. It wasn't until this case was featured on television that the people of this community realized they had had a fugitive for their doctor for nearly two years.

Emergency Response Teams

Even the Mounties need help in emergencies. When they can't handle a situation they call their own specialists, the Emergency Response Team (ERT). These teams usually consist of eight to ten Mounties, a dog handler and a police service dog. These expert teams help during hostage-taking situations, plan assaults, provide backup when needed and much more.

There are about 30 ERTs across Canada. Members train two days a month, in addition to all their regular duties. They practise target-shooting using many types of guns, act out responses to dangerous situations and work out to keep incredibly fit. One member of each ERT is a sharpshooter.

ERTs also take part in drug raids. They grab suspects before they can escape, then guard them while the drug squad searches for drugs. Some ERTs have the dangerous job of boarding ships suspected of carrying drugs. What's so difficult about that? The ships are usually moving at top speed and the ERTs board them by rappelling down from helicopters!

A Mountie is polite, brave, strong and always gets his man, right? That's certainly the image that movies, books and TV give the members of the Force. Take the show *Due South*, for instance. Every week, Mountie Benton Fraser fights crime on the streets of Chicago with his faithful sled dog, Diefenbaker.

Your parents probably remember shows such as *North of 60*, *The Beachcombers* or *Bordertown*, which featured Mounties. And before TV, Sergeant Preston of the Yukon, Dale of the Mounted and many others were on radio fighting evil doers.

If you want to read about Mounties, try *Inuk Mountie Adventure* by Eric Wilson. Did you know that both Wilson and author Sheree Fitch have Mounties for dads?

Interpol

Despite what you see in the movies, there are no Interpol detectives who jetset around the world catching criminals. The International Criminal Police Organization, or Interpol for short, helps police forces all over the world work together to put an end to international crimes. These crimes include smuggling drugs and weapons, terrorism, counterfeiting and theft of everything from ancient Egyptian treasures to modern art.

In each country around the world, one police agency coordinates and responds to all Interpol inquiries; in Canada, this agency is the RCMP. The National Central Bureau, known as Interpol Ottawa, is located at RCMP Headquarters in Ottawa. One of Interpol Ottawa's jobs is to investigate tips from people who have something to report after watching TV shows such as *America's Most Wanted* and *Unsolved Mysteries*.

Auxiliary Police

Next time you see a group of Mounties, take a look at their hats. Most probably have the yellow hatband of a regular member, but if you see a hat without a yellow band, it belongs to an Auxiliary Constable. These are volunteers who are taught about making arrests, enforcing traffic laws, handling prisoners, giving first aid and CPR, and more. Almost 2500 Canadians have completed this special training.

Auxiliary Constables join regular members on routine patrols, where they can help in many ways, such as directing traffic around accidents. Some adults who have been accepted into the RCMP cadet program volunteer as Auxiliary Constables while they are waiting to begin Mountie training.

Other Auxiliary Constables already have other jobs but want to serve their community or add a little excitement to their lives. Teachers, church ministers and librarians have all served as Auxiliary Constables. People who want to be associated with the RCMP but can't leave their home town often volunteer. Being an Auxiliary Constable can be an exciting way to learn about the RCMP.

WHEN IS A MOUNTIE NOT A MOUNTIE?

Everyone who works for the RCMP is a Mountie, right? Wrong! Of the 22 000 people who work for the Mounties, about one-third are civilians. Some are typists and secretaries, while others are experts in forensics or telecommunications.

Other experts who are civilian members of the RCMP include pilots, doctors, psychologists and physiotherapists. For example, in the past many of the pilots for the Force were regular members of the RCMP, but now most are civilian members. As well, psychologists work with Mounties to help them cope with stressful situations they've experienced. These include being involved in a shooting or when members return from United Nations policing duties in Haiti. The Force is trying to keep the people they have trained as police doing police work and to have fewer police doing administrative or other types of work.

One civilian who reached the top ranks of the RCMP is Mireille Badour. Between 1994 and 1996 she was a Deputy Commissioner, the second-highest rank in the RCMP. Badour was the first woman to achieve this honour.

As Deputy Commissioner, Corporate Management, Badour was in charge of all of the Mounties' money. Badour managed a budget for the Force and made sure that there was enough money to carry out all of the Force's programs.

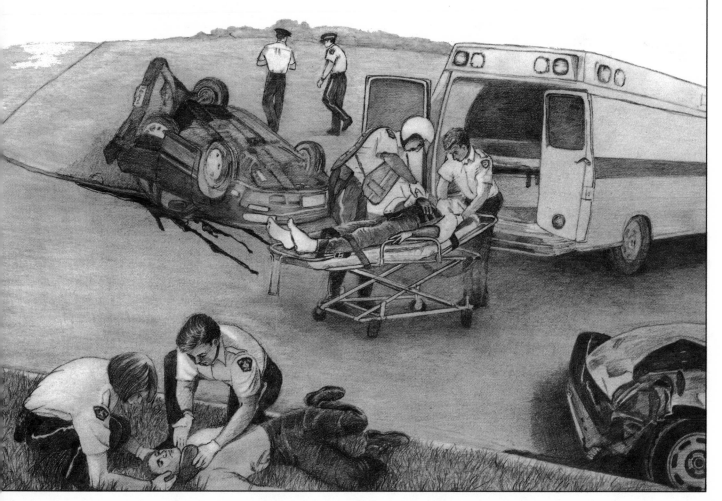

Undercover Work

The bar is in the roughest part of Montreal. Dark, smoky and crowded, it's a hang-out for drug dealers, addicts, criminals, bikers and loan sharks. John Warren eyes the other people in the bar intently — he wants to find someone who will sell him drugs. Warren spots several people who he thinks are drug dealers but he hesitates. These people are tough and will take his life in an instant if he says the wrong thing.

But Warren is lucky. Soon he has what he wants and heads out of the bar to his friends, who are waiting in a car. The driver quickly pulls out of the parking lot — and heads for the nearest RCMP detachment. What?! Warren and his friends are going to proudly show the Mounties all the drugs they bought tonight. That's because John Warren and his buddies are really Mounties working undercover. Buying drugs from suspected traffickers in bars is a test all Mounties go through as part of their undercover training.

Undercover Mounties sometimes work on simple cases, such as catching criminals red-handed by buying drugs from them. Or they may be involved in long-term investigations that involve waiting for a suspect to make a drug deal. In some projects, a team approach is used: one Mountie gets to know a suspected drug dealer, learns what illegal things he is doing and tries to catch him when he makes a big drug deal. Other Mounties are close by and ready to come to his aid when he needs it. The RCMP works with other police forces, sharing information and giving and receiving help when the undercover operation moves out of the RCMP jurisdiction or area.

Sometimes a suspect under surveillance will do something unexpected, such as go to an airport and get on a flight. There's no time for the Mountie to call a superior for instructions, so he has to act fast — buy a ticket, get on the plane and keep following the suspect. Some undercover Mounties have found themselves suddenly on a plane to England or India while following a suspect. This travel can cost a lot, but it could also lead to the arrest of a suspect as he attempts to bring $1 million worth of drugs into Canada.

Not everyone agrees with what undercover agents do. For instance, they sometimes pay criminals for information that is used to catch other criminals. Or while undercover, Mounties may try to buy drugs from people who will break the law if they sell the drugs to the officer. Many people feel that it's wrong for police to trick someone into committing a crime and then arrest her. What do you think?

Help — Send a Mountie Right Away!

Listen in as RCMP radio operators respond to calls from people in trouble:

Line 1: "… Calm down. Now I'll repeat that slowly back to you to make sure I've got the exact location of the accident. Turn at the first gas station on Route 7 west of town … There should be an officer there shortly and I'll contact the ambulance immediately."

Line 2: "… It sounds like there is a fight going on in the background. I understand someone there may be preventing you from talking, but if you need help, just say yes. However, you'll have to tell me your location so that I can dispatch officers to come help you."

Line 3: "… Stay where you are and we'll have an officer there soon."

RCMP telecom or radio operators take phone calls from the public, assess the situation, then radio the nearest officer. Operators must calm people in crisis so they can get the information they need, then send the right kind of help.

The operator is the link between the RCMP and the public. As well, when a Mountie responds to a call, the operator monitors her movements to keep the Mountie safe — the operator is the Mountie's lifeline and Mounties depend on this help.

Radio operators help Mounties in other ways. When a Mountie stops a car for speeding, she often radios for information about the driver and the car. The radio operator will access the Canadian Police Information Centre (CPIC) computer system to see if the person is a wanted criminal or if the car has been stolen.

If a driver who's pulled over is from outside of Canada, the radio operator may contact Interpol or the FBI to find out more about the person. The public — and the Mounties — can feel safe knowing that help is only a radio call away.

EARLY USES OF THE RADIO

The Mountie brought his car to a screeching halt and dashed into the restaurant. "Turn on that radio!" he commanded.

That might have been the scene back in 1938 in Saskatchewan. Twice a day, Mounties on patrol would listen to radio station CKCK for bulletins about missing or wanted persons, stolen cars, etc. Since police cars didn't have radios, Mounties had to make sure that at 10:35 a.m. and 3:50 p.m. they were at a restaurant, gas station or someone's home listening to the radio.

By late 1939, police cars were being equipped with radio receivers. Mounties could now hear the messages from their own cars, but they still couldn't respond. During the 1940s the RCMP began developing its own radio network and equipping police cars and RCMP detachments with two-way radios.

Now the Mounties' communications network is one of the largest non-military mobile communications systems in the world.

CHAPTER SIX

THE NEXT 125 YEARS

The seller looked nervous, and her story about why she was selling the painting was too vague. "And I'm almost certain Arden de Pompadour isn't her real name," gallery owner Christine Bowes said to herself.

Aloud, she said, "I'd like to buy this painting, Ms de Pompadour, but your price is too high. If you care to lower it, please contact me." De Pompadour said she'd be in touch and quickly left. *I wonder if I can find out more about her on my computer*, thought Bowes as she watched de Pompadour leave.

Bowes accessed the RCMP's World Wide Web site on the Internet. She wasn't sure where to look but tried the page featuring Canada's most wanted criminals. Suddenly, Bowes gasped. "There she is! She's a big-time drug dealer. And I was right — her real name isn't Arden de Pompadour, it's Pamela Wilson! I'll bet that painting is stolen."

Quickly Bowes called the RCMP and spoke with Constable Nick Carter, an expert on stolen art. Bowes described the painting and Carter confirmed that it was stolen. "We've got to catch Wilson and put her out of business," said Carter. "If you'd bought the painting and resold it to one of your customers, you would have unknowingly sold stolen property," he explained. "The painting might eventually be seized from your customer, and everyone, except the thief, would be out a lot of money."

Bowes agreed to let Carter work in her gallery and pose as her assistant. It wasn't many days before Wilson returned. She said she wanted to give Bowes another chance to purchase the painting. The deal was made and then Wilson got a shock! Carter showed her his RCMP identification and told her she was under arrest.

Wilson confessed to Carter how she obtained the stolen painting. With this information the RCMP made more arrests and discovered that the stolen painting was part of a plan to finance a drug deal in Vancouver.

Thanks to Bowes and the RCMP's Web site, a thief was caught, the painting was returned to its owner and fewer drugs ended up on Canada's streets.

Technology Catches the Criminal

"This guy's driving much too fast. He's going to kill someone! I'm going to have to harpoon him," says Constable Hope Alexander as she activates the Mounties' latest technology. Attached to the front of her police car is a Carpoon, a barbed device like a huge harpoon. Alexander aims it at the trunk of the car in front of her, shoots it, then applies her brakes to stop the speeding car. She can spray tear gas into the car if the driver locks himself in. Sound impossible? It's already a reality in Finland and may be used someday by the RCMP.

Advanced technology is already helping to catch criminals and will be used even more in the future. For instance, could a detail as small as a suspect's chipped front tooth help convict a killer? Definitely, if a suspect in another murder case also had a chipped front tooth and if this information had been entered on ViCLAS — the Violent Crime Linkage Analysis System.

To use ViCLAS, an investigator of violent crimes answers more than 250 questions about an event. The computer uses this data to try to link the crime with others already posted and come up with a possible suspect. Answering the questions is time-consuming, but if all police enter their data about violent crimes, more criminals will be caught faster.

The RCMP is also researching the use of DNA (deoxyribonucleic acid) typing. DNA is the part of every cell in your body that determines the characteristics, such as eye and hair colour, that you inherit from your parents. DNA typing is done using blood,

saliva or even the root of a hair and can prove that a suspect was at the scene of the crime or free a person who's wrongly accused.

DNA testing is expensive and can take several weeks to complete, so it is only used for cases of violent crime. As the tests become cheaper and quicker, it may be used for a larger variety of crimes.

In the future, the government may allow police to collect blood for DNA analysis from everyone convicted of a violent crime. Police could search this data to try to solve crimes at which suspects had left body fluid.

As scientists learn more about DNA they may be able to use it to create a physical description of an individual. The police of tomorrow could use an eyelash found at a crime scene to generate a picture of a suspect!

MOUNTIES ON-LINE

You can use the technology of today to browse the RCMP's World Wide Web site, just as gallery owner Christine Bowes did. The Internet address is

http://www.rcmp-grc.gc.ca

At this Web site you can view wanted criminals, enter a contest to name Musical Ride foals, read about police dog services, visit an RCMP forensic lab and find out about many other aspects of the RCMP.

If you have a fax machine, you can learn more about the RCMP by phoning their "Fax-on-demand" line at 1-888-RCMP-GRC. Follow the directions to have specific information faxed to you.

Community-Based Policing

If you and your friends walk to school along a street on which there's lots of traffic, what can your parents do if they become concerned that some of those cars are driving too fast in an area with a lot of kids? One thing they can do is talk to the local Mounties.

The RCMP wants to work with citizens, local government and community groups to make people feel safe in their homes and in their communities. It's called community policing. Mounties are working with all segments of their communities to define priorities for the police in the local detachments.

Anyone — high-school students, seniors, business people — can let the Mounties know what's on their minds by joining a Community Consultative Group.

The RCMP also has programs that allow kids to learn more about what Mounties do. The School Liaison Program sends Mounties into schools to talk to kids and help with programs such as Students Against Drunk Driving (SADD) and bike rodeos. As well, anyone aged 14 to 26 can join the RCMP Venturer or Rover program; this would be of interest to anyone considering a career as a Mountie. University students can also be Special Constables and spend their summers working with the Mounties.

Mounties Around the World — United Nations Policing

When Haiti wanted to improve its police force, it contacted Canada and was soon working with the RCMP. Before the RCMP arrived in Haiti, shooting was the first reaction of many of the local police. But thanks to a United Nations program run by the Mounties and other police from around the world, the Haitian police are learning to handle dangerous situations without violence.

Mounties also work for the United Nations as civilian police monitors in countries such as Namibia and the former Yugoslavia. Their duties include working with local police, as they're doing in Haiti; helping people displaced from their homes by war; and monitoring elections to ensure they are conducted fairly and properly.

DISTRICT POLICING

Have you been seeing more RCMP cars on the highways lately? Because of reorganizing called district policing, Mounties are spending more time patrolling highways and sitting in their police cars. It may look as if they are trying to catch speeders, or maybe even eating doughnuts, but actually the Mounties are completing reports on laptop computers or using their cellular phones to update people who have had property stolen or have reported other crimes.

By organizing a group of RCMP detachments into a district, fewer officers are needed in the office, which saves money, gets more Mounties out on the road and probably gets them to crime scenes faster.

Controversy and the RCMP

Mounties used to make headlines because they caught dangerous criminals. But recently the RCMP has been in the news more and more because of controversy and protests. For instance, in 1989 Commissioner Norman Inkster decided to allow Mounties to wear religious symbols, such as turbans, as part of their uniform. This allowed men who practise the Sikh religion, and who are required to always wear a turban, to join the RCMP.

This decision upset many people. They believed that if someone wants to be a Mountie then he should wear the uniform without changes. But in February 1996 the Supreme Court of Canada ruled that changing the RCMP uniform to accommodate religious beliefs is legal. The first Mountie to wear a turban with his uniform was Constable Baltej Dhillion.

In 1995 the RCMP began another national debate by signing an agreement with the Disney corporation. Walt Disney (Canada) Ltd., a branch of the giant American company, now decides which companies can use the RCMP image on products. This means that a company that wants to print a picture of a Mountie on something, such as a mug or a T-shirt, has to work with Disney. It also must pay a fee that is split between the Mounted Police Foundation (MPF) and Disney.

Nothing Goofy about RCMP deal

RCMP launches attack on unlicensed 'kitsch'

Disney wins right to market Mounties

DISNEY DOGS

When Mounties first patrolled the North by dogsled they used local dogs. But these semi-wild dogs were very vicious, so in 1960 the Mounties started breeding their own sled dogs. Twenty of these dogs were donated from a Walt Disney movie, *Niki: Wild Dog of the North*. Descendants of these Disney dogs pulled Mountie sleds until 1969, when the RCMP switched to snowmobiles. Check your library or video store for a copy of *Niki*.

Many Canadians were furious that a part of Canadian history was now controlled by a giant American corporation. The Mounties insisted that Disney has a reputation for quality products and that the RCMP would maintain control over what sort of products will be produced. There was much confusion about exactly what the deal would mean.

The confusion even affected the book you're reading right now and caused controversy that was front-page news. Do facts about the RCMP belong to the Force or are they part of Canadian history? This book almost didn't get published because, at first, Disney and the MPF wanted to be paid for the information you're reading and wanted to approve everything in this book. But eventually Disney agreed that a book about the Mounties is not something they control as part of their deal with the RCMP.

The five-year deal between the MPF and Disney should earn the RCMP $25 million and earn Disney even more. With that money the RCMP will support many programs, including a drug awareness program at Davis Inlet, Slave Lake Victim Services Society in Alberta and New Brunswick Crime Stoppers.

So You Want to Be a Mountie

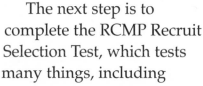

Now that you know more about the RCMP, maybe you think you'd like to join up. The first step is to attend an information session about becoming a Mountie. These sessions are open to anyone who:

- is at least 19 years old
- is a Canadian citizen
- has graduated from high school
- speaks either English or French
- has a driver's licence
- is healthy
- is honest and reliable
- is able to keyboard at least 19 words per minute
- is trained in first aid and CPR

The next step is to complete the RCMP Recruit Selection Test, which tests many things, including language skills and the ability to observe and recall details. Another test, the Physical Abilities Requirement Evaluation (PARE), includes a simulated chase, struggle and arrest.

The next hurdle is a three-hour interview that asks everything from whether the candidate has ever used illegal drugs to how she feels about the possibility of shooting someone. The purpose of the interview is to find out if the applicant is emotionally stable, why she wants to become a Mountie, and how she will adapt to police life and the strict discipline of life as a cadet. The RCMP method of screening applicants is tougher than for any other police force in Canada. That's probably why the RCMP has a low drop-out rate compared to other forces.

Applicants who speak both French and English are tested on their second language. Next the candidate fills out a detailed personal history, including information about family, friends, employers, teachers and neighbours. The Mounties interview many of these people to find out about the applicant's past.

The last step is medical and dental exams. After a wait of anywhere from a few months to a few years (the average wait is about a year), applicants learn whether they've been accepted by the RCMP.

Each year approximately 10 000 people apply to become Mounties, but only about 600 are selected. The maximum number of cadets that can be trained each year is 768, or 32 troops of 24 cadets. Once a person is accepted for cadet training, she reports to the RCMP Depot Division in Regina to begin 26 weeks of basic training (see pages 10 to 15). Cadets who complete basic training are then hired on as members of the RCMP. After reaching this final step, the new Mountie will be a proud member of one of the most famous police forces in the world.

INDEX